With walls, walls, a global malaise,

of concrete, and digital haze.

AI's cold stare,

Indoctrination's snare,

And tariffs that muddle our days.

Prologue

Walls are no longer only physical. They now are also part of VR, invisible. The toughest barrier to cross is indoctrination - toxic, not easy to vanquish.

Traces of Nazism linger; Fascism is on the rise. So is bigotry. A different kind of colonization is happening. Plutocracy occupies the throne. The cold war is back. WW III looms.

The goal of zero unemployment will, according to the richest man on the earth, fall by the wayside, replaced by Zero employment. Employment will become the cherished hobby of the elite.

That is not Dystopia, but Utopia.

This book is a not even a feeble whisper.

Let us hope, in the year of Hope, that the whisper is not silenced.

Preface

This book is divided into four walls, in sync with the acronym **WAIT**, formed from the first letters of the four walls that are discussed in the pages that follow:

Section 1: Walls, Physical

This section is the longest, starting with a visual history of some walls of infamy, followed by a few short stories of the plight of innocent people most impacted by walls.

Section 2: AI Walls (Platform Domination)

This section critically examines the economic, social, and political implications of artificial intelligence (AI) and big data, positioning them as key instruments of capitalism rather than as neutral technological advancements.

Section 3: Indoctrination Walls

"Propaganda is where a demagogue plays pedagogue and starts a monologue to leave their audience agog." – **Stewart Stafford**

This section explores the human mind, while capable of extraordinary feats of creativity and empathy, is susceptible to the construction of invisible yet formidable barriers: mind walls.

Section 4: Tariff Walls

This section explains what tariffs are, the history of tariffs and tariffs' devastating impact on the economies of nations, especially developing economies, and the scars protectionism leaves.

Physical Walls

Walls Mart

The Great Wall of China

A grand, ancient stone wall stretching over mountains, resembling the Great Wall of China during the Ming Dynasty. Soldiers in traditional armor patrol the wall, with banners fluttering in the wind. The misty atmosphere adds a sense of historical depth and grandeur.

Hadrian's Wall

A historic Roman-era stone wall stretching across rolling hills, resembling Hadrian's Wall in Britain. Roman soldiers in red tunics and helmets patrol the wall, while a small wooden fort stands nearby. The lush green landscape and cloudy sky add to the dramatic setting.

The Berlin Wall

A Cold War-era concrete wall dividing a city, resembling the Berlin Wall in the 1960s. One side of the wall is covered in graffiti and protest slogans, while the other side has armed guards patrolling with watchtowers. A dimly lit street and barbed wire add to the tense atmosphere.

The Maginot Line

A World War II-era fortress wall with bunkers and turrets, resembling the Maginot Line in France. The structure is made of reinforced concrete, with large gun emplacements facing outward. The surrounding landscape is a mix of grass and barbed wire, with a cloudy war-torn sky overhead.

The Korean Demilitarized Zone (DMZ)

A heavily fortified border zone with barbed wire
fences, watchtowers, and armed soldiers, resembling
the Korean Demilitarized Zone (DMZ). The scene is
tense, with military checkpoints and a distant view
of a divided land. The foggy atmosphere adds to the
sense of separation and conflict.

The Israeli West Bank Barrier

A tall, concrete separation wall resembling the Israeli West Bank Barrier. The wall is covered in graffiti, with watchtowers spaced along its length. A military checkpoint with soldiers is visible, and a Palestinian neighborhood can be seen on one side, contrasting with a modern cityscape on the other.

The U.S.-Mexico Border Wall

A long, steel border wall stretching across a desert
landscape, resembling the U.S.-Mexico Border Wall.
A group of people stand on one side looking toward
the other, while a border patrol vehicle drives
nearby. The scene is dry and arid, with mountains in
the background and a dramatic sunset casting long
shadows.

The stories that follow, it is hoped, will generate empathy and compassion, love, generosity, caring and sharing.

The Crack

Leila and Samir grew up in neighboring villages, their affection blossoming across a river that marked the boundary between their countries. When a conflict erupted, a towering wall was built, dividing not just land but hearts. They would meet at the wall, whispering through the cracks, their fingers barely touching through the cold concrete.

Years passed, and the wall grew taller, guarded by indoctrinated soldiers who saw love as a threat. One day, Samir stopped coming. Leila learned he had been arrested for trying to climb the wall. She realized the wall wasn't just made of bricks—it was built on fear, propaganda, and hatred. She began writing letters, not just to Samir, but to others on both sides, urging them to see beyond the lies that divided them.

The wall was not just physical; it was a symbol of the fear and lies that kept people apart.

Love and truth could dismantle it, brick by brick.

A Mother and Daughter Apart

Amina raised Zara in a small, close-knit community, but when Zara turned 18, she joined a religious cult that preached isolation from the "corrupt" world. The cult built walls—literal and figurative—around its members, cutting them off from family and friends. Amina tried to reach Zara, but the cult leaders turned her away, calling her an "outsider."

Years later, Zara escaped the cult, her mind scarred by years of indoctrination. She returned to her mother, who welcomed her with open arms. Together, they worked to help others break free from the mental walls that trapped them.

The hardest walls to tear down are the ones built in the mind. Resilience and love can help us overcome even the deepest indoctrination.

Siblings on Opposite Sides

Karim and Tariq were inseparable as children, but as adults, they found themselves on opposite sides of a political divide. Karim joined a revolutionary movement, while Tariq became a loyalist, believing the government's propaganda. A wall was built in their city, dividing neighborhoods and families. The brothers stopped speaking to each convinced the other was brainwashed.

One day, during a violent clash, Karim was injured. Tariq, now a soldier, found him bleeding on the ground. In that moment, the ideologies faded, and they were just brothers again. Tariq carried Karim to safety, realizing the walls between them were built on lies.

Political and ideological walls can divide even the closest of families. Only by seeing each other as human can we break them down.

Friends Across the Fence

Maria and Sofia grew up playing together in a small town that was later split by a border fence. Maria's family stayed on one side, while Sofia's moved to the other. As they grew older, the fence became a symbol of their separation. They would meet at the fence, sharing stories and dreams, but the divide grew wider as their governments fed them opposing narratives.

One day, Maria brought a pair of wire cutters. Together, they cut a small hole in the fence, just big enough to hug. They realized the fence was not just a physical barrier—it was a tool to keep them from questioning the lies they were told.

The fences we build are often meant to keep us from seeing the truth. Resilience and courage can help us tear them down.

The Wall of Silence

Ahmed and Yusuf lived in a country where dissent was punished. When Yusuf joined a protest movement, Ahmed, fearing for his safety, begged him to stop. But Yusuf refused, and the government built a wall to separate the "troublemakers" from the rest of the population. Ahmed was forbidden from seeing his son.

Years later, Ahmed found a letter Yusuf had smuggled out. It spoke of hope and resilience, urging people to resist the lies that divided them. Ahmed realized the wall was not just physical—it was a tool to silence truth. He began speaking out, breaking the wall of silence that had kept him apart from his son.

Silence and fear are the real walls that divide us. Only by speaking out can we break them down.

AI Walls

AI: Technology Walls and Platforms

Author's note: The author gratefully acknowledges the startling revelations of Bhabani Shankar Nayak & Nigel Walton in their book **Political Economy of Artificial Intelligence: Critical Reflections on Big Data Market, Economic Development and Data Society** (6 September 2024)

The book critically examines the economic, social, and political implications of artificial intelligence (AI) and big data, positioning them as key instruments of capitalism rather than neutral technological advancements. It argues that AI is reshaping labor markets, economic structures, and governance while reinforcing corporate monopolies, exacerbating labor precarity, and threatening democratic principles.

Insights:

1. The Data-Driven Society & AI's Role:
    AI and big data are central to modern economic structures, functioning as tools for capitalist expansion.

The emergence of a "data society" shifts the traditional means of production, replacing land, labor, and capital with data and information. This transformation has deep social implications, affecting governance, citizenship rights, and economic participation.

2. AI, Capitalism, and Labor Exploitation:
    The traditional Marxist labor theory of value is on shaky foundations.
    AI-driven economies create a "neo-bourgeois" class of platform owners and a "neo-proletariat" of data providers.

3. Platform capitalism, where companies like Google, Amazon, and Alibaba dominate, restructures traditional labor dynamics, often leading to labor instability and precarious employment.

4. Big Data as a Market Commodity: o AI-driven digital platforms manipulate big data as a new form of capital, influencing market structures and consumer behavior.

5. The rise of monopolistic data-driven platforms challenges conventional economic models, necessitating new policy frameworks to regulate AI and protect labor rights.

6. AI's Political and Geopolitical Implications: o AI is a key battleground in global power struggles, particularly between China and the U.S., as they compete for technological supremacy.

7. Surveillance capitalism and digital authoritarianism are emerging threats, influencing governance models and eroding democratic participation.

8. Future Challenges & Policy Considerations:

AI threatens citizenship rights through increased surveillance, algorithmic bias, and digital exclusion;

Policies that ensure ethical AI deployment, labor rights protection, and equitable economic benefits;

The risks of AI singularity and the loss of human agency in a fully automated society;

Conclusion:

A critical global political economy perspective on AI is called for. Unchecked AI-driven capitalism can run amuck, deepen social inequalities and create tech monopolies. Policymakers need to regulate AI's economic role, ensuring the seamless integration of sustainable goals and ethical integration into society.

Indoctrination Wall

Indoctrination Wall

The Foundation of Mind Walls

Indoctrination, the process of instilling beliefs or doctrines uncritically, forms the bedrock of these mental barriers. It suppresses independent thought, replacing it with rigid adherence to a prescribed worldview. From early childhood, individuals may be exposed to biased narratives, selective information, and emotional manipulation, shaping their perceptions of the world. This process can occur within families, religious institutions, and, most insidiously, through state-controlled media and education systems. Indoctrination creates a sense of "us versus them," where dissenting opinions are not merely different but inherently threatening.

Bigotry: The Mortar of Prejudice

Bigotry, the intolerant prejudice that fuels discrimination, acts as the mortar that binds the bricks of mind walls.

It thrives on fear and ignorance, categorizing individuals based on superficial characteristics like race, religion, or sexual orientation. Bigoted beliefs are often rooted in stereotypes and misinformation, propagated to justify hatred and exclusion. These beliefs create a distorted reality where "others" are dehumanized, stripped of their individuality, and perceived as a monolithic threat. Bigotry solidifies mind walls by creating emotional barriers, preventing empathy and fostering hostility.

Fascism: The Architectural Blueprint

Fascism, the authoritarian political ideology, provides the architectural blueprint for constructing these imposing mental structures. It exploits existing prejudices and anxieties, offering simplistic solutions to complex problems.

Fascist regimes utilize propaganda, censorship, and surveillance to control information and suppress dissent, reinforcing indoctrinated beliefs.

They cultivate a cult of personality around a charismatic leader, demanding unquestioning loyalty and obedience.

Fascism thrives on division, creating scapegoats and enemies to rally support and justify oppressive policies. It erects mind walls on a societal scale, isolating entire nations and fostering a climate of fear and intolerance.

The Consequences of Mind Walls

The consequences of these mental barriers are devastating:

- **Erosion of Empathy:** Mind walls prevent individuals from understanding and connecting with those who are different, leading to dehumanization and violence.

- **Suppression of Critical Thinking:** Indoctrination stifles intellectual curiosity and the ability to question established narratives, hindering progress and innovation.

- **Social Division:** Bigotry and fascism fracture communities, creating deep divisions that fuel conflict and instability.

- **Authoritarianism:** The control of information and suppression of dissent create an environment ripe for authoritarian rule, where individual freedoms are sacrificed for the perceived security of the state.

Tearing Down the Walls

Overcoming these mind walls requires a conscious and sustained effort:

- **Education and Critical Thinking:** Promoting education that emphasizes critical thinking, media literacy, and exposure to diverse

- perspectives is essential.

- **Dialogue and Empathy:** Fostering dialogue and understanding between different groups can break down stereotypes and build bridges of empathy.

- **Challenging Bigotry:** Actively challenging bigoted beliefs and behaviors is crucial to creating a more inclusive and tolerant society.

- **Protecting Freedom of Expression**: Upholding freedom of expression and access to information is vital for countering indoctrination and holding power accountable.

Mind walls, though invisible, are powerful forces that shape our world. By recognizing their existence and actively working to dismantle them, we can create a more just, compassionate, and understanding society.

Tariff Walls

Tariff Walls

Tariffs create barriers between countries primarily by increasing the cost of imported goods. This has a range of effects that can impact trade relationships and the broader economy. Here's a breakdown:

How Tariffs Create "Walls":

Increased Prices:

Tariffs are essentially taxes on imported goods. This directly raises the price of those goods for consumers and businesses in the importing country.

This price increase makes imported goods less competitive compared to domestically produced alternatives.

Reduced Trade:

As imported goods become more expensive, demand for them tends to decrease. This leads to a reduction in the volume of trade between countries.

This can disrupt established trade relationships and supply chains.

Protectionism:

Tariffs are often used to protect domestic industries from foreign competition. By making imports more expensive, they give domestic producers a price advantage.

However, this protectionism can also lead to inefficiencies, as domestic industries may become less incentivized to innovate and improve.

Retaliation and Trade Wars:

When one country imposes tariffs on another, the affected country may retaliate by imposing its own tariffs.

This can escalate into a "trade war," where both countries impose increasingly higher tariffs, further hindering trade and creating significant economic disruptions.

Distorted Markets:

Tariffs can distort market forces, causing resources to be allocated inefficiently. They can artificially inflate the price of goods, which can cause consumers to pay more for goods than they would in a free market.

Tariffs act as a financial barrier, making it more difficult and expensive for goods to cross borders.

This can lead to decreased trade, strained international relations, and potential economic harm.

It's very helpful to look at real-world examples to understand how tariffs impact international relations and economies.

Here are a couple of key case studies:

1. The 2018-2019 U.S.-China Trade War:

What happened:

The United States, under the Trump administration, imposed tariffs on billions of dollars' worth of Chinese goods, citing unfair trade practices and intellectual property theft.

China retaliated with its own tariffs on U.S. products.

This led to a prolonged period of escalating tariffs, impacting a wide range of goods.

Effects:

Increased costs for businesses and consumers in both countries.

Disrupted supply chains, forcing companies to find alternative sources for materials and finished goods.

Increased uncertainty in the global economy.

Strain on the relationship between the two countries.

2. Historical Examples and the concept of "Limes"

Roman Empire:

The Roman Empire's construction of "limes" (fortified borders) served not only as physical barriers but also as customs checkpoints.

While these walls had a defensive purpose, they also regulated the flow of goods and people, effectively creating trade barriers.

The economic burden of maintaining these defenses, combined with other factors, contributed to the empire's eventual decline.

Demonstrates how physical barriers can also function as economic barriers. Shows that heavy investment in trade restriction can have negative long term economic effects.

Tariffs often lead to retaliatory measures, creating a cycle of protectionism that harms global trade.

While tariffs may protect certain domestic industries in the short term, they can also stifle innovation and reduce competitiveness in the long term.

The impact of tariffs can vary depending on the specific industries involved and the overall economic climate.

Epilogue

2025 Declared as The Year of Hope

These stories remind us that the walls we build - whether physical or ideological - are marketplaces of division, where ideologies, fears, and lies are traded. They are not insurmountable.

The true barriers are the ones built in our minds by those who seek to control us. Resilience, love, and unity are the tools we need to dismantle these walls and create a world where hope prevails.

In the Year of Hope, let us remember that the walls we face are not made of bricks, but of fear and lies. Together, we can tear them down and build a future rooted in truth and unity.

Let us not succumb.

www.ingramcontent.com/pod-product-compliance
Lightning Source LLC
Chambersburg PA
CBHW040218110726
48005CB00019B/3068